THE 100 BEST
KITCHENS & DINING ROOMS

BETA-PLUS

THE 100 BEST
KITCHENS & DINING ROOMS

CONTENTS

Restoration of a 17th-century convent farm 6

Contemporary yet timeless 10

A romantic country house. 12

Respectful renovation of a private mansion. 14

Contemporary living on the Scheldt 16

Warm minimalism 18

Sober refinement in a contemporary penthouse. 20

Contemporary transformation of a country house kitchen. 22

An intimate atmosphere 24

A new home 26

Transparency, openness and geometry 28

Space and light in harmony 30

A worthy successor 34

A harmonious whole in a timeless setting 36

A very tasteful B&B 38

Perfect harmony 40

A large and spacious duplex penthouse. 42

The timeless beauty of white Carrara marble 44

The timeless kitchen of a classic manor house. .46

In French style 48

Irresistible charm 50

The splendour of wood 54

A perfect balance 56

Sober refinement in a classic French manoir 58

A perfect blend. 60

Lightness and luminosity 64

A functional kitchen with pure lines 68

A contemporary kitchen in a restored farmhouse 70

An understated holiday home in Ramatuelle. 72

Simple sophistication in high-tech surroundings. 76

A sense of space 78

Flemish style 82

A tasteful renovation of a historic notary's house 84

A blend of timeless and contemporary: a balanced philosophy for living. 86

A gentle renovation. 90

Space and subtle luxury in a sculptural villa. 92

Understated elegance 94

Sophisticated simplicity in a distinctive country home 96

A loft with a breathtaking view of the capital 98

The transformation of a former workshop into a modern home 100

A residence in Cape Cod. 102

A kitchen in old stables. 104

Magnificent surroundings 108

The contemporary kitchen of the Ommerstein castle. 110

A magnificent view 112

The art of living on the Côte d'Azur 114

Carte blanche. 116
In the heart of the city 118
Purity, light and restraint 120
A true holiday feel 122
A kitchen in bleached and sandblasted oak. 124
A timeless manor house kitchen 128
Warm ambience, contemporary style 132
Inviting. 136
Minimalist and monochrome 138
A true metamorphosis. 142
As though risen from the ashes 146
Traditional craftsmanship. 148
A perfect balance 150
A view of the sea. 152
All in one: kitchen, library, dining and living room 154
The kitchen as the centre of the home. 156
A passion for design and fine quality 160
A pure philosophy for kitchen and home design 164
Horizontality and clear-cut lines 166
A specialist in high-quality kitchen work surfaces. 168
A distinctive new villa in wooded surroundings. 170
An open orangery kitchen cum dining room 172
A unique atmosphere 174
A passion for natural stone 176
Perfection in custom-fitted natural stone 178
Shades of green 180
Old and new. 182
The real centre of the house 184
The revival of a 19th-century castle 186
Freshening up a restored farmhouse 188
Renovation of an 18th-century mill 190
Creating the perfect kitchen 192
Colonial inspiration 194
Reliable and functional. 196
Authentic charm. 198
Exclusive kitchens with a contemporary edge. 200
The kitchen as the core of a home-design concept. 204
The cooker as the heart of the kitchen 206
Creativity and craftsmanship 210
Bianco statuario in the kitchen 214
The restoration of the historic Cretenburghoeve 218
Episcopal inspiration 220
Anno 1642 222
Intimate and cosy. 224
Minimalism and contemporary art 226
A perfect ergonomy 228
A recently built country house with an age-old patina 230

RESTORATION OF A 17TH-CENTURY CONVENT FARM

This enclosed convent farm, situated in Flemish Brabant, was built in the seventeenth century with a double wall: one around the farm buildings and one around the farmyard. The low-lying farmhouse was in a very bad state of repair. The house, consisting of two floors and seven bays, the stables and the barn, the gatehouse and the small service buildings were all restored very thoroughly and adapted by architect Bernard De Clerck. The moat was dug out, the grounds were laid out according to the old model and supplemented with new rows of trees. The canals have been deepened. Antiques and decoration: Garnier. Reclaimed materials: Rik Storms.

info@bernarddeclerck.be

The "upstairs room", the special room where guests and friends are received for elegant dinners.

The washing-up area in the large kitchen.

The kitchen with a view through to the flower garden.

CONTEMPORARY YET TIMELESS

Tack Entr. have made a name for themselves in recent years as leading designers and manufacturers of high-quality kitchens built according to tradition in a classic, contemporary style. Frank Tack has also developed a unique concept of simply designed contemporary and yet timeless interiors, constructed in wood and stone: the perfect proof that modern designs do not have to feel cold. The look is always created to fit the space and to be in harmony with the existing architecture. Design and functionality go hand in hand, sometimes pushing the limits of technical feasibility. Every plan is designed to the specifications of the client and finished according to their wishes. Each project is unique. The interaction of colours and light is studied very carefully. Professional advice is absolutely essential for this aspect of the design.

www.tack-keukens.be

A spacious, functional island for washing-up and working. with facing sinks and a separate breakfast corner.

A simple design with straight lines still gives off a feeling of warmth. The correct proportions ensure balance and calm.
The ceiling-height doors were cut from one piece. The washing-up island has been equipped with a professional tap. The doors have an ecological finish and are heat-, shock- and scratch-resistant. The sliding cupboard units allow for considerable ease of use. Lighting in function of this kitchen space.

↖
The space has been opened up to form a balanced whole consisting of light and dark tints. Door surfaces in specially selected pin oak. The dining-room table harmonises with the rest of the design.

A ROMANTIC COUNTRY HOUSE

This kitchen is located in the heart of a country
house created by the Costermans firm.
It's the favourite meeting point for
all members of the family.

www.costermans-projecten.be

A rustic gas cooking ring by the French brand Delaubrac, an elevated gas fire, attractive fitted cupboards in French oak, a display case with wrought-iron doors, a sturdy dining table with comfortable chairs: a place to cook, to have lunch or to have dinner and linger at the table afterwards.

RESPECTFUL RENOVATION OF A PRIVATE MANSION

A 19th-century private mansion in Brussels was renovated with respect for
the historical character of the premises by Jos Reynders Decor and decorated
by Helena van den Driessche, in close collaboration with the owners.

www.fahrenheit.be   www.reynders-goc.com

CONTEMPORARY LIVING ON THE SCHELDT

A young self-employed couple gave interior architect Bert Van Bogaert
carte blanche to design and create a stylish, strictly minimalist loft
for them with a breathtaking view of the river Scheldt.
The generous budget meant that only high-quality materials were used, and it
was possible to devote attention to the finish of even the smallest details.
The kitchen has been designed and realized by Interieur De Maere.

bert.vanbogaert@pandora.be   www.interieurdemaere.be

The loft faces south and the large windows allow in plenty of light. The whole project was designed to be as empty and spacious as possible.

The kitchen appliances are concealed behind hinged and sliding panels.

WARM MINIMALISM

A family with growing teenage daughters exchanged life in the city for the leafy outskirts, finding a beautifully situated location for construction in the middle of woodland. Architect Michal Muylaert translated the desires of the clients – light, space, peace and a great sense of openness, combined with sufficient privacy for the residents – into a sober, timeless architecture with a blind façade and a glass rear wall that looks out onto the garden and woods. The spaces flow seamlessly into one another, but ceiling-height doors and sliding partitions can create separate rooms and privacy if needed. Involving architects and interior designers (Koen Aerts, Pas-Partoe and Kultuz) in the project right from the beginning has resulted in a great sense of harmony between the colours, materials, light and proportions. This blurs the boundary between inside and outside and creates a real feeling of space.

www.michelmuylaert.be

The furniture was carefully selected and comes mainly from the collections of Minotti and Piet Boon.

↖
The open kitchen was designed by the owners of the house as an extension of the living room. The cupboards are in dark-grey stained oak and the surfaces are in lava stone. Cooker-hood filters, indirect lighting and loudspeakers are incorporated into the canopy above the counter.

SOBER REFINEMENT
IN A CONTEMPORARY PENTHOUSE

Devaere, an interior-design studio from West Flanders, designed and created this spacious penthouse. Nico Devaere discreetly integrated all the technology required for modern comfort (such as domotics and air-conditioning systems) into this contemporary design: all of the elements form a united whole with the interior and the architecture of the building.

www.devaere-nv.be

Plain shapes combined with
distinctive, fine materials:
central block and work
surfaces in Brecchia marble,
floor in Pierre de Varennes and
matt varnished furnishings.

↖
This picture clearly shows
the open character of the
dining room,
the living area
and the kitchen.

CONTEMPORARY TRANSFORMATION
OF A COUNTRY HOUSE KITCHEN

A country house, built in 1970 by architect Librecht, has been transformed into a
contemporary living space by the current owners, a family with three children.
The Brussels interior architecture and design agency InStore created the new
interior, including the sober yet warm kitchen and dining area.

www.instore.be

A dining table (model Dumbo)
and chairs (model Brigitta)
from Promemoria. A Charles
couch from B&B Italia.

↖
Flexform chairs (model
Mixer) in this kitchen with
its professional Viking
cooker.

AN INTIMATE ATMOSPHERE

Costermans built this classic country house in the green countryside surrounding
Antwerp. Historic building materials were used consistently throughout the
project, lending the house a timeless and intimate atmosphere.
The spacious kitchen has sleek units in thick French oak veneer. Floor
in bluestone laid in broken bond. The stove is by Delaubrac; the work
surface is in smoothed bluestone. Taps by Perrin & Rowe.

www.costermans-projecten.be

The dining room has the same warm and intimate atmosphere. The eye-catching piece in this room is the impressive crystal chandelier.

The sinks are in solid stone and the edges of the work surfaces have a hand-cut finish.

A NEW HOME

This newly built house is the cosy home of a family with five teenage daughters. This decidedly modern and timeless building blends perfectly with its wooded surroundings. The Reginald Schellen architectural studio prefers to work on projects such as this, where the aim is an integral approach to interior and exterior. Light and space play a central role in the studio's designs. Creating seamless connections between inside and outside is one of the studio's central credos: for this reason, interior architect Linda Coart was involved in the project right from the beginning.

www.schellen.be   www.lindacoart.be

The central block with its granite work surface dominates the room. This block extends to form a large breakfast table. The American refrigerator and cooker hood are beautifully integrated in a painted facing wall.

TRANSPARENCY, OPENNESS AND GEOMETRY

This recent project by Pascal François is a fine example of the virtuosity with which this architectural studio based in Aalst is able to create practical minimalism. The result is an open living area, offering lots of garden views and with skylights and large windows ensuring plenty of light.

www.pascalfrancois.be

The kitchen is based around the same kind of concrete unit.

The cooking alcove with recessed cupboard units and a cooker hood.

SPACE AND LIGHT IN HARMONY

A young couple with three children built this luxurious house, together with Crepain Binst architectural studio. They called upon the services of 'aksent for the complete interior design. It was important that the clean, modern lines of the apartment should not become too chilly and cold. Stefan Paeleman from 'aksent took a contemporary approach that differs significantly from the normal designer look. The words 'past' and 'future' were important themes here. In line with the philosophy of their favourite design firm Promemoria, the link with the past ensures a sense of calm, whilst the future brings excitement and expectation.

www.aksent-gent.be

The window with slightly smoked glass provides a view of the staircase.

The table and benches are a design by Stefan Paeleman for 'aksent. Dark oak and bronze have been combined to make the table; the cushions on the benches are upholstered with a horsehair fabric by Le Crin.

↖
The designers chose a natural stone for the kitchen that matches the materials used outside. The wengé doorframes create a link with the floors in the rest of the house. The cooker hood has been completely integrated into the ceiling so as not to form a visual obstruction in the room.

A WORTHY SUCCESSOR

Joris Van Apers continues his father's tradition: he has a large collection of beautiful reclaimed materials: antique fireplaces, old timber floors and natural stone slabs, ... But he also introduces a new dimension to the family business: the antique construction materials are incorporated into complete projects, with techniques for patination and ageing. The result: a most harmonious look in a timeless setting, with top-quality materials, traditional techniques and a large dose of creativity and technical know-how. The kitchen in this report is a good illustration of the company's unique approach.

www.vanapers.be

A view of the kitchen. This wall cupboard is made up of parts of an antique piece of furniture and has an age-old patina.
Sink and work surface in French natural stone, produced in the company's own workshop.
The door is in old, weathered "cheeseboards".

The cooking area with an extractor integrated into the 18th-century fireplace, a work surface around the hob in pigmented, polished concrete and handmade, anthracite-grey doors. On the floor, old Burgundy slabs in free bond. The wall tiles are Dutch "witjes". The kitchen island consists of 18th-century planks, two original doors and an aged red marble surface.

A HARMONIOUS WHOLE IN A TIMELESS SETTING

This second kitchen project by Joris Van Apers (the first is shown on pages 34-35) is another example of his virtuosity: integrating architectural antiques and old patination techniques into a harmonious whole in a timeless setting.

www.vanapers.be

Original Dutch tiles on the wall. White-beige «tomettes» on the floor.

A floor in old Carrara marble.

A VERY TASTEFUL B&B

The owners discovered this farmhouse on an overcast day in May. It was not an obvious choice as somewhere to go and live, but they dreamed of life in the country and saw nothing but prospects in the farmhouse's dilapidated state. When the restoration was carried out, the conscious decision was taken to go for a contemporary approach, involving all the materials being cleaned up and all mod cons being incorporated. Integrating the surrounding landscape into the residence as much as possible was one of the explicit tasks facing architect Gerd Van Zundert, who has succeeded extremely well in doing just that.

www.moka-projects.com   www.moka-vanille.com

The kitchen with AGA cooker is the central place where friends are greeted. There's no designer furniture here, but old items of furniture that the client has picked up on her trips to jumble sales and which give the room certainty.

↖
The art of simple domesticity has been perfected in the kitchen. The basis here consists of terracotta ware fired in a reduced atmosphere, whitewashed walls and a free-standing display-case unit.
Like the worktop, the sink was hewn from a single block of solid blue Belgian limestone and runs through into the windowsill.

PERFECT HARMONY

This kitchen has been designed and realized by Bourgondisch Kruis.
The bluestone for the kitchen tops, the washbasin, the walls and the work zone
behind the cooker are in perfect harmony with the planks in old oak.
The floor is clad with old bluestone slabs (50x50 cm).

www.bourgondisch-kruis.be

A LARGE AND SPACIOUS DUPLEX PENTHOUSE

This duplex penthouse on the Belgian coast is unusual in many respects.
This is a very large apartment with both the charm and floor space
(over 1000m²) of a country house, but with a unique sea view.
The home has been finished to a very high standard throughout. Obumex designed
and created the ground floor, while interior architect Philip Simoen was responsible
for the design of the upstairs rooms, which were then created by Obumex.

www.simoeninterieur.be   www.obumex.be

The kitchen was designed and built by Obumex.

Dining area with a Lloyd Loom table and JNL chairs.

THE TIMELESS BEAUTY
OF WHITE CARRARA MARBLE

Costermans created a kitchen in a contemporary apartment block:
a restful and understand ambience in white Carrara marble.

www.costermans-projecten.be

The contemporary kitchen with its Italian Carrara marble floor, surface and wall. Custom-cut tiles were selected for the floor, so as to minimise the number of joints.

THE TIMELESS KITCHEN OF A CLASSIC MANOR HOUSE

In a newly built villa in manor style, Themenos created
an exceptional and very spacious kitchen.

www.themenos.be

IN FRENCH STYLE

Over recent years, Costermans has built up a solid reputation as a construction company for exclusive villa projects. The house in this report, built in a French style, is a good example of Costermans' working methods: the use of durable materials throughout, together with enthusiasm, skill and a strong focus on the interior, with a timelessly classic design.

www.costermans-projecten.be

The kitchen, in French oak, is equipped with all mod cons. Surface in pale-brown French limestone: the wall tiles are hand-made Moroccan zelliges. The panel doors are made of French oak.

IRRESISTIBLE CHARM

Antique dealers Brigitte and Alain Garnier rebuilt their tumbledown
stable to make a unique, very spacious kitchen and dining area.
This kitchen demonstrates the sophisticated way in which this husband-and-
wife team combine exclusive antique pieces in all of their interior projects
with historic building materials that radiate an irresistible charm.

www.garnier.be

A floor made from 18th-century oak planks: Brigitte Garnier was concerned about the maintenance of the floor, but even after a great deal of use it has proved to be most durable and easy to look after.

Floor in red and black Boom tiles.

The mudroom is clad with wooden cheeseboards.

The old staircase leads to a guest room.

On the rear wall, an 18th-century deux-corps dresser (height: 3.6 m) with the original patina. Unit with Italian pasta block (240x200 cm). Italian walnut-wood shutters discreetly separate the kitchen from the room behind.

THE SPLENDOUR OF WOOD

This open kitchen has been designed by architect Bernard De Clerck.
The floor is covered with 19 cm large oak planks by Corvelyn.

info@bernarddeclerck.be   www.corvelyn.be

An oak parquet floor with
19cm-wide planks has been
laid in this kitchen and
dining area.

A PERFECT BALANCE

Benedikte Lecot is an interior designer who aims to create a symbiosis of functionality, atmosphere, light and architecture in all of her projects. She aims to achieve a unity of style within a pleasant living environment that balances classic and modern, and which is always in keeping with the individual needs and desires of the client. All of her designs are therefore created à la carte. The exclusive character of her interiors is further reinforced by perfect workmanship, carried out by experienced and passionate professionals. Benedikte Lecot is involved with most projects from the earliest structural work on the building: this means that she can easily take into account small details that will be important during later stages.

www.b-lecot.be

The extra-wide oven is integrated into a ceiling-height wall-unit. The cooking island stands in a central position.

↖
Wooden chairs and a
painted bench around a long
refectory table.

SOBER REFINEMENT
IN A CLASSIC FRENCH MANOIR

This classic French manoir in the leafy outskirts of Antwerp was constructed by Costermans.
The company devoted the utmost attention to the selection of materials, installing unusual
antique tiles, durable old parquet floors, exceptional fireplaces and other special details.
The look is timeless, yet contemporary: a sober and sophisticated living environment.

www.costermans-projecten.be

A timeless, solid-oak kitchen in combination with a hand-painted pine table. The work surface is in a grey French natural stone. The cooker is the Provençal model from the French company Delaubrac. The wall tiles behind the cooker are hand-made Moroccan zeliges.

↖
Various forms of ironwork: windows, dresser doors and the antique gate to the wine cellar.

A PERFECT BLEND

Interior Architects Brigitte Boiron and John-Paul Welton continue their cooperation further and provide the complete renovation of this apartment of 320 m² located in a historic building in Geneva. They created a timeless and luxurious universe that will honour their art collection, a wish of the residents. The company Project Design was responsible for the complete renewal of the rooms. Under the leadership of Brigitte Boiron the decoration became a perfect blend of the many works of art and the custom-made furniture. John-Paul Welton shows his expertise: the creation and implementation of a part of the furniture, autographed by Welton Design. Knowledge of materials, subtlety of tone on tone colours and the grey tints provide a refined and warm living environment. Contrary to tradition, the entrance of the apartment is a spacious reception area with a high and long table and a recreational area, furnished with a sofa in cowhide, where you can enjoy a drink or watch the cook's preparations...

www.projectdesign.ch   www.weltondesign.com

In the hall. a carpet in cowhide by Miyabicasa an oak parquet floor. A bar furniture and 8 leather tabourets with a chromium base, all from the Welton Design collection.

Elitis wallpaper in the kitchen finished with stainless steel and tinted oak. Parquet floor in oak.

↖
«Louvre» chairs by Balthus around a dining table autographed by Welton Design. An «Atlantis» chandelier by Terzani and a silk carpet by Diacasan. 100% silk curtains by Henri Bertrand in a silver colour. A crocodile sculpture by Richard Orlinski (numbered edition). The Barbie installation is a creation by Louis Boiron. A photographic work «The Secret» by Greg Miller. Two compressions in chromium on the chimney. A sculpture from Cambodia (16th century). A sculpture «Born to be Wild» by Richard Orlinski.

An Arche bar table
and eight tabourets
(Welton Design).
A bronze hanging
lamp (Pia
Promemoria).
Refrigerators,
deep-freezers and
wine coolers are by
SubZero.

The kitchen
was made in
stainless steel
and black tinted
oak by Arclinea -
Ambiance Cuisine.

LIGHTNESS AND LUMINOSITY

Located on top of a promontory, this villa was completely restructured "feet in the water» style, and enlarged by GEF Réalisations, the office for interior design. Transparency, lightness and luminosity were the keywords in this project. The interior design, which is extended outdoors and in the garden, was subtly designed by landscape designer Loup & Co., who extends the architectural reflex to the sea.

gef@wanadoo.fr   www.loupandco.com

The kitchen, made of stratified wood and grained quartz, is open to the lounge and dining room. The circulation is free-flowing.

A FUNCTIONAL KITCHEN WITH PURE LINES

In this apartment designed by interior architect Simone Kengo (Minimal Interior) Obumex created a very practical kitchen with pure and simple lines.

www.obumex.be   minimalinterior@skynet.be

All kitchen furniture is made of tinted oak by Obumex. A Viking cooker.

A CONTEMPORARY KITCHEN
IN A RESTORED FARMHOUSE

When renovating this initially unpromising farmhouse and barn in Flanders, architect Vincent Van Duysen strived to maintain the serene and homely rural character of the house. So, the emphasis in the interior was subtly placed on the country surroundings. Purely to emphasise the spatial qualities, he introduced some large windows looking onto the modest, green garden. With the simple interplay of views, circulation axes and different ceiling heights, the architect creates a fascinating space that does not fall within everyday expectations. The sober, yet warm choice of colours and materials reinforces this effect.

www.vincentvanduysen.com

The dining room with its solid elm table by Vincent Van Duysen.
The chairs are by Christian Liaigre. The faded pastel colour palette of the hand-woven and naturally tinted linen is in tune with the colours of the garden.

AN UNDERSTATED HOLIDAY HOME IN RAMATUELLE

Christel De Vos (De Vos Projects) created this newly built villa in
Ramatuelle, in collaboration with Nathalie Mousny.
The house was given a stucco finish and painted white; only
the roof tiles reveal a Provençal inspiration.

www.rrinterieur.be

The Bulthaup kitchen with Botticino work surface and stools designed by Bataille + ibens.

The dining room with a table designed by Vincent Van Duysen in solid elm. Chairs by Christian Liaigre.

SIMPLE SOPHISTICATION
IN HIGH-TECH SURROUNDINGS

The owners wanted a practical, extremely comfortable home: bright, simple and cosy, with
lots of natural light and made of basic, but very reliable materials. The same materials
were used throughout: dark natural stone for the floor and the washstand in the cloakroom;
tinted and brushed oak veneer for the cupboards and solid-oak parquet flooring.
The lighting also plays an important role, and a great deal of attention was paid to
the latest technology in audio and video, lighting control, security, video phones and
air conditioning with touch-screen operation, internet and specially made key panels
(designed and created by Dubois Ctrl – air conditioning and automation concepts).

www.stephanielaporte.be   www.obumex.be   www.christian-liagre.fr   www.duboiscontrol.be

Chairs by Christian Liaigre around a Promemoria table (both from Obumex).
The walls have been finished with a special stucco painting technique. Gunther Lambert pots.

↖
Natural stone, oak veneer
and stainless steel are
combined in the kitchen.
An integrated cold store.
Blinds by Bruder.

A SENSE OF SPACE

This magical place, situated in the heart of Brussels, has a view that certainly stands comparison with any metropolis. It used to be an office space on the roof of a residential building, but it has now been converted into a wonderful apartment with a garden and terraces and a floor area of 500 m². The apartment was designed by Nathalie Delabye for Ensemble & Associés and furnished throughout by Isabelle Reynders with creations by Christian Liaigre. In consultation with the client, who is just as enthusiastic as the designers about the "invisible" details, this space has been transformed into a place where purity and simplicity harmonise with a real sense of well-being.

www.ensembleetassocies.be   www.christian-liaigre.fr

The kitchen was designed by Ensemble & Associés and built by Obumex.

↖
Work surface and central
cooking area in Unistone
composite stone and units in
white-stained sandblasted
oak. Specially made cooker
hood in Stadip metal and
brushed stainless steel.
Stools designed by Claire
Bataille.

FLEMISH STYLE

Architect Stéphane Boens was inspired by the classic Flemish farmhouse for this project. The kitchen is very inviting with its open fireplace and the central unit.

www.stephaneboens.be

Harmony of old beams and large slabs in reclaimed bluestone.

A TASTEFUL RENOVATION
OF A HISTORIC NOTARY'S HOUSE

This notary's house dates from 1807. The exterior and interior of the building are both listed.The main building has all the charm of a grand, historic home. The extensions, designed by Stéphane Boens, have a more country feel and are completely integrated into their surroundings. Authenticity and simplicity were the most important principles in this project. White was therefore an obvious choice as the basic colour, as it emphasises the pure and beautiful character of the space.

www.stephaneboens.be

The kitchen walls are clad in old Dutch white tiles.
The floor is an old restored cement floor.
A white Aga stove and old Provençal chairs in combination with 18th-century chairs from am projects. A staircase is concealed in the wooden section, which leads to the children's playroom.
The old oak table has built-in power points and is for eating and working on.

↖
The kitchen units all have old, original doors. An old pump trough with a work surface, both in bluestone.

A BLEND OF TIMELESS AND CONTEMPORARY:
A BALANCED PHILOSOPHY FOR LIVING

This farmhouse was created by architect Stéphane Boens.
The owners also use the house as a showroom for am projects, their interior-design company.
Their work is more a philosophy of life than simply decoration.
They create timeless environments and living spaces that are perfectly in balance
with the lifestyle of their clients. They decorated this house themselves.

www.amprojects.be

A Viking cooker for this kitchen designed by am projects. The floor is covered with bluestone slabs.

↖
In the kitchen-cum-dining room are two Dutch chandeliers made to an 18th-century design. The glassware is also based on an old design.

A wing chair upholstered in pale-blue linen.
The elm table on trestles is based on an antique design.

A GENTLE RENOVATION

The passionate lady of the house renovated her country
estate in a very meticulous and respectful way.
It was a gentle renovation, keeping all authentic architectural elements intact.
The kitchen is surprisingly contemporary, yet in perfect harmony
with the timeless interior and architecture style.

The spacious kitchen-cum-dining room is built around a central cooking island.

↖
The bleached-pine table is over four metres long.

SPACE AND SUBTLE LUXURY
IN A SCULPTURAL VILLA

Custom-built interiors are Obumex's area of unmatchable expertise. This house, designed by the
Brussels architect Fabien Van Tomme, is an example of the company's approach. The garden
and surroundings are by Buro Groen. Xavier Gadeyne, senior interior architect at Obumex,
designed and supervised all of the interior work. Sumptuous materials, subtle colours and
impressive spaces make this home and office a place of luxury and relaxation. Complemented by
modern art from the owner's collection, this house forms a timeless and contemporary whole.

www.obumex.be

The dining table was designed and created by Obumex, combined with black-tinted Y chairs by Hans J. Wegner.

The kitchen is a John Pawson by Obumex design.

UNDERSTATED ELEGANCE

A rather dull French-style house from the 1960s was transformed to create a spacious, up-to-date home that fulfils all of the client's requirements for comfort. Light and (breathing) space were key elements of this design. So as to allow the house to develop more character, hardwood that will evolve naturally with the surroundings was selected for the windows. Materials that develop a patina over time are also a feature of the interior. This means that the house will lead a life of its own and the aesthetic qualities of the space will increase. The roof was also thoroughly remodelled in order to create more space. This whole upper storey can now be used optimally. The alterations even made it possible to install a mezzanine floor in the rooms of the two teenagers. The sense of calm and understatement in this home is remarkable. 'Aksent have turned their philosophy into reality in this strong combination of functionality and emotion.

www.aksent-gent.be

The kitchen is called Quatre4, a link to the use of four different types of wood. The architectural look of the kitchen unit is reinforced by the details of the work surface.

SOPHISTICATED SIMPLICITY
IN A DISTINCTIVE COUNTRY HOME

Husband-and-wife team Alain and Brigitte Garnier fitted out this attractive
country house in a timeless style that is casual and sophisticated at the
same time. Verraes Decoratie carried out the painting work.

www.garnier.be

French terracotta tiles on the kitchen floor and black Moroccan zelliges on the wall.
A wrought-iron candle chandelier and Le Manach blinds by Garnier.

A LOFT WITH A BREATHTAKING VIEW
OF THE CAPITAL

This loft, situated on the top floor of a converted industrial building, has
been completely reorganised by interior architect Anne Derasse.
The central room consists of a long rectangle with cross
beams dividing the space into six bay sections.
All of the functions flow together in the same space.
The entire space and the fitted furniture were designed by Anne Derasse.

www.annederasse.be

The other side of the kitchen block is a polished oak sideboard that conceals the kitchen work surface.
The tall units have the appearance of elements that have been stacked on top of one another.

THE TRANSFORMATION OF A FORMER WORKSHOP
INTO A MODERN HOME

The architectural studio Julie Brion and Tanguy Leclercq A.D.
managed the complete transformation of this former workshop in a
lively part of Brussels to create a modern house of 250m².
The design is very sober and streamlined: gentle minimalism in soft shades.

www.brionleclercq.com

A view from the kitchen into the open space of the dining room and sitting room.

A RESIDENCE IN CAPE COD

The owners of this house asked Bruce Bananto (New York City), to design the extensive architectural interior as well as the interior design of this newly constructed house which is idyllically situated beside an exclusive golf course in Mashpee, Cape Cod. The exterior and general layout was designed by a local architect Doreve Nicholaef (Osterville, Massachusetts). The look is timeless and contemporary: the combination of interesting finds from Europe, locally hand crafted furniture designed by Bruce Bananto and constructed by Michael McGuire and a series of well-chosen works of art by Joan Sonnabend ensure that this home has a universal appeal.

www.bananto.com

The dining room is situated next to the kitchen.

↖
A decidedly modern oven
in stainless steel and a
natural-stone work surface
in Absolute Black.

A KITCHEN IN OLD STABLES

This beautiful long-fronted farmhouse, one of architect Raymond Rombouts' unique creations, has recently been renovated by interior architect Alexis Herbosch (Apluz design studio). At the request of the owners, an extension was built and the interior of the farmhouse completely renovated. Alexis Herbosch and the owner (both keen enthusiasts of Rombouts' work) worked together to achieve harmony between the existing house and the extension. The harmony of the proportions and the use of materials resulted in a complementary whole: it looks as though the extension has always been there.

www.herbosch-vanreeth.be

The kitchen was rebuilt in the stables.
To recreate the original atmosphere of the rear facade, two existing
windows were replaced by a new oak stable door.
Old tumbled bluestone was chosen for the floor.

MAGNIFICENT SURROUNDINGS

Vlassak-Verhulst, the exclusive villa construction company, built
this stately country house with a number of outbuildings.
The house, situated in magnificent natural surroundings near Bergen aan
Zee (Dutch coast), was then handed over to Sphere Concepts, who assumed
responsibility for the entire design and creation of the interior.

www.vlassakverhulst.com   www.sphereconcepts.be

A table in reclaimed old oak
and custom-made lampshades
in plissé linen.

The back kitchen in solid oak.
A washbasin made to measure
in Buxy cendré natural stone.

↖
The cooking area with a
stainless-steel cooker and a
work surface in composite
stone.

THE CONTEMPORARY KITCHEN
OF THE OMMERSTEIN CASTLE

The Ommerstein Castle has been thoroughly restored by the Simoni design office in collaboration with Scoop. The castle itself has no historic value. In the course of time it was renovated, the roof construction was in a sorry state and the interior had become very undistinguished. It was decided to dismantle the castle almost completely and to start the design process all over again. As the customer wanted a luxurious furnishment a modern design with a certain classic elegance was chosen.

www.simoni.be   www.vandenweghe.be

The kitchen is definitely contemporary, with natural stone works by Van den Weghe. Floors, walls and the work unit were finished with Pietra Piasentina stone.

A MAGNIFICENT VIEW

This site is a triangular plot that was part of an older parcel of land. It is situated on a busy approach road, but at the same time offers a magnificent view of the attractive rural surroundings. These were key factors in this design by Hans Verstuyft Architects.

www.hansverstuyftarchitecten.be

THE ART OF LIVING ON THE CÔTE D'AZUR

Commissioned by a property developer, RR interior Concepts took this newly built villa in Saint-Tropez completely in hand. In this project Christel De Vos concentrated entirely on the complete furnishing and finishing. Both for outside and inside the furniture selected came from Flexform, B&B Italia, Minotti, Maxalto,… The object was to create a pleasant environment where the surroundings and the finished interior form a single united whole.

www.rrinterieur.be

Fresh colours, in combination with a black contrast, show a controlled vision. This is an example of the art of living outside the Belgian frontiers; a challenge from which RR Interior Concepts certainly did not shrink.

CARTE BLANCHE

Interior architect Guillaume Da Silva was given a free hand for this project: the reinterpretation and renovation of an old village school. The original building, which in the course of years had undergone many transformations, had lost much of its attraction, but large volumes of space promised a strong residential potential. The classroom was transformed into a drawing room. Fascinated by the quality of light within the building Guillaume Da Silva used this source to create volumes with pure lines. The guideline is white, which fits everything. Materials were treated with chalk, the oak floor was bleached. The course concrete was given a bath...

www.guillaumedasilva.com

All the furniture for this unique project were selected by RR Interior Concepts: Groundpiece sectional sofas by Flexform, lacquered armchairs Jenny, a big white massive wooden table designed by Vincent Van Duysen and chairs by Walter Knoll.

IN THE HEART OF THE CITY

The Brussels design company Ensemble & Associés were asked to fit out a 200m² apartment in the heart of Brussels. The key words were: open, calm, pure. Luxury of space, superiority of materials and quality of finish: these three elements are of prime importance to Ensemble & Associés in all of their projects.

www.ensembleetassocies.be

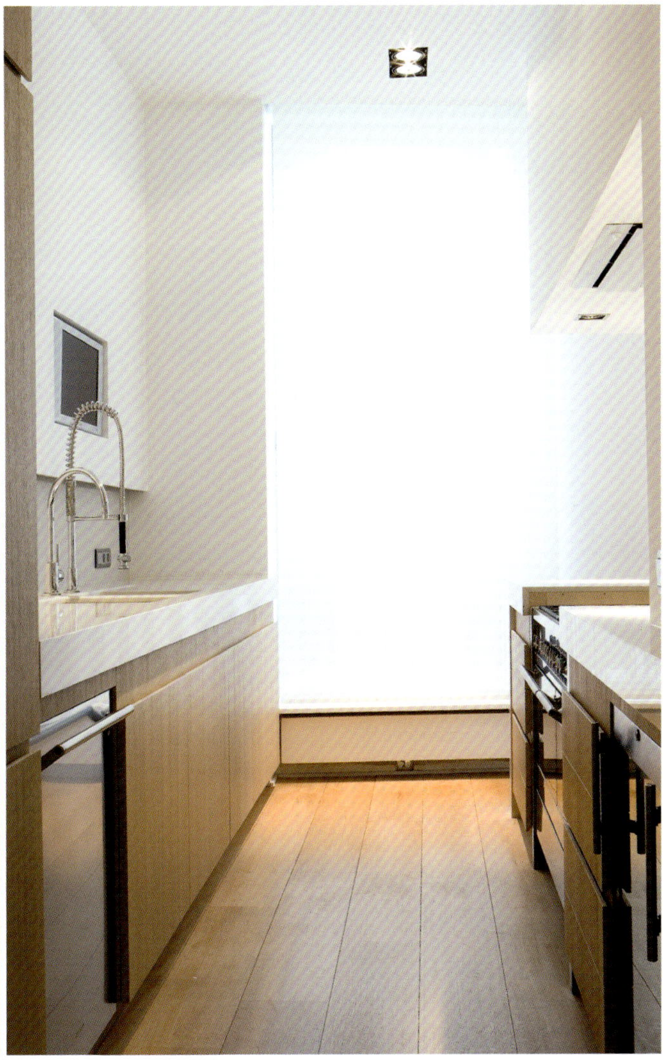

The panels of the storage cupboards have been
given a white-lacquer finish. Shelves in bleached,
sandblasted oak. Furniture: Luz Interiors.

PURITY, LIGHT AND RESTRAINT

The challenge for this apartment from the 1960's: creating an
oasis of calm and wellbeing, with a sea view.
Purity, light and restraint were the key words in this project.

www.ensembleetassocies.be

The kitchen was finished in grooved, white varnished MDF.
Work surface and wall in Negro Tebas composite stone.

A TRUE HOLIDAY FEEL

For this home, idyllically situated in Walloon Brabant, the challenge was to
reconcile a wooden building structure with a contemporary interior.
A successful project: when you enter this home, you are overwhelmed by a true holiday feel.
Architect: Gregory Dellicour. Building contractor: Mi Casa.

www.ensembleetassocies.be

The kitchen was entirely designed by Ensemble & Associés and realised in sandblasted oak. The composite stone work surface has been bevelled to 45°.

A KITCHEN IN BLEACHED AND SANDBLASTED OAK

This kitchen is part of a design by Ensemble & Associés.
There is a view of everything from the kitchen ... the living room, the dining
room and the family room, all designed in neutral, soft shades.

www.ensembleetassocies.be

The kitchen was designed by Ensemble & Associés and finished in sandblasted,
bleached oak and Crema composite stone. Taps by Dornbracht.

The library is also a design by Ensemble & Associés, realised in sandblasted and bleached oak. CH24 chairs by Hans Wegner and a table by Carl Hansen.

A TIMELESS MANOR HOUSE KITCHEN

Within a setting of lovely park trees, Costermans Villa Projects realised a timeless English manor. The architectural design and use of materials have strong English roots.

www.costermans-projecten.be

A rustic oak table looks out at the garden. During the winter, an antique Louis XV fireplace ensures comfortable warmth.

The spacious kitchen-diner has a comfortable atmosphere: a large oak work island forms the heart of this space. The cabinets are all made of solid oak panel doors combined with wrought-iron windows and grips.

WARM AMBIENCE, CONTEMPORARY STYLE

Atelier Vincent Bruggen realizes about twenty houses in
Canadian wood skelet construction a year.
The kitchen in this report is part of their most recent success stories: everything
has been custom built by the professional team of Vincent Bruggen.

www.vincentbruggen.be

The kitchen is realized by Atelier Vincent Bruggen (Diepenbeek).
The kitchen floor is covered with honed Carrara white marble in 60x80 cm tiles.
The table-top is made of two 360 cm long boards.

The ceiling in Oregon pine and the boards give the kitchen (with a Viking cooker) a somewhat rural character.

INVITING

This house, situated in one of the most beautiful streets in Antwerp, was seriously renovated with respect for the distinctive original architecture and for the valuable materials that were very much worth preserving.

www.costermans-projecten.be

In the kitchen, a central work block with a solid worktop in French whitestone was chosen in harmony with the natural stone floor covering of diverse French origin. The use of natural materials combined with the furniture and the window decorations make this an inviting space for family and friends.

MINIMALIST AND MONOCHROME

This classic house had a traditional layout with closed rooms and an incorrect location as regards to the garden and the swimming pool. The interior architecture agency Minus was given the task to open up the space and maximise contact with the environment. The pure design, with axes on the windows, ensures that the residents can always look outside from one space through the other. The whole has a lavish look and is yet simple, with natural materials and ton-sur-ton colour palette.

www.minus.be

The kitchen was constructed around a cooking, washing and sitting section, with closed walls. The volume in high gloss paint, the walls in structure paint and the work surfaces provide a subtle contrast.

A TRUE METAMORPHOSIS

A rustic villa with a lot of oak and dark materials was transformed by Peter Ivens (interior and architecture agency Astra Loves Living) into a modern country residence: the residence experienced a true metamorphosis through a few strong interventions.

www.astralovesliving.com

The kitchen in the new annex. The central island is covered with a granite monolith from the company Tondat.
The side of the cooking niche in black oak is covered with black zelliges. The flooring in Pietra di Medici, a rough stone with an open structure.
The new whole was furnished with vintage furniture (Items, Knokke).

AS THOUGH RISEN FROM THE ASHES

The Brabant farm in this report appears to have been standing for centuries, but appearances can be deceptive: this country house was completely constructed with old building materials by architect Stéphane Boens. Boens took inspiration for this project from the authentic eighteenth-century farmhouses that were common in Walloon Brabant: a long driveway leading to an entrance gate that would open out on to an inner courtyard with a main building and several outbuildings.

www.stephaneboens.be

A central block with rinsing sinks has been placed in the contemporary classic country kitchen.

TRADITIONAL CRAFTSMANSHIP

De Menagerie is a company specialising in the design and creation of custom-built kitchens. These designs are created on the basis of close consultation with the clients. Key to their approach is the aim for balance and the synthesis of the architectural space with functionality and aesthetics to create a unique whole. These kitchens are built completely by hand, using traditional techniques, with the focus on the high quality of the materials and finish. This results in a very personal look that harmonises beautifully with the atmosphere of the house and the lifestyle of its owners.

www.demenagerie.be

The Aga stove and the raised fireplace make this a very cosy home.
The MDF drawers and doors have no handles and have been given a white paint finish. Work surface in solid 5cm-thick bluestone, with a rounded edge.

A PERFECT BALANCE

In this spacious country house, De Menagerie found a perfect balance
between the functional character of the kitchen and its conviviality.

www.demenagerie.be

A VIEW OF THE SEA

The interior design of this seaside apartment with a magnificent sea view
was created by Stefanie Everaert and Caroline Latour (Doorzon).
Obumex's senior interior architect Tom Sileghem took care of
the technical engineering and the site supervision.
The Van den Weghe stone company carried out all of the stonework.

www.doorzon.be   www.obumex.be   www.vandenweghe.be

ALL IN ONE: KITCHEN, LIBRARY, DINING AND LIVING ROOM

This report illustrates the architect's mission to bring a 1960s house into line with modern living and working habits, whilst, as far as possible, retaining the original volumes and architecture. The divisions between the different rooms within the space have been removed, improving the circulation throughout the house. One large space was created over the entire length of the house so as to incorporate the garden into the living area. This space contains the dining room, kitchen, living room and library.

www.ravestyn.be

A view of the newly created dining
room with the long table and
gas fire as central elements.

↖
A view of the kitchen and
dining room, as seen from
the living room. The table
and the cupboard
units beside the fireplace are
custom-made.
The table forms the central
visual point of the dining
area.

THE KITCHEN AS THE CENTRE OF THE HOME

Mape is a family concern that has specialised in the production of kitchens and bathroom furniture for over forty years. The architecture, ergonomics and functionality of the kitchen are at the heart of every project: the kitchen is an essential element of the living environment. All of the lacquering work is carried out in the company's own workshops and is of the highest quality. The extensive kitchen range can be selected in different materials: from MDF with a high-gloss or matt finish to solid natural or synthetic materials. All of the kitchens are developed by Mape's design team from the basic plan to create a unique design that corresponds perfectly to the wishes of the client.

www.mape.be

A streamlined kitchen in MDF with a white matt finish and no door furniture.
The central island is equipped with a rectangular sink and Dornbracht
taps, and is also used as a table: it can seat four people.
The contrast of the dark oak floor with the white units and walls
lends a sober and serene appearance to this kitchen.

↖
The alcove containing the
cooking surface has sliding
doors. These cupboards
provide practical storage
space for small pieces of
electrical equipment.

The work surface, in harmony with the large floor tiles, is in 5cm-thick smoothed bluestone, with two square sinks in the same material. Taps by Dornbracht. The cooking area consists of a flat induction plate and an extractor built into the plain MDF canopy, which has been painted to match the ceiling.

This custom-made kitchen is in solid aged oak. The doors have no handles and are built from three layers of material for optimal stability. The Amana refrigerator has been completely integrated into the wall unit. The wood grain runs horizontally on the drawers and pull-out cupboards, emphasising the impression of length. All of the drawers and pull-out cupboards are equipped with fully telescopic, silent runners.

A PASSION FOR DESIGN AND FINE QUALITY

Driven by a passion for techniques and home interiors, the De Keyzer family has
been producing kitchens with pure and timeless designs for thirty years.
Creativity and craftsmanship are at the centre of all of their projects: the additional selling
points of this kitchen-design company are the luxurious details and the incomparable finish.

www.dekeyzer.be

The cooking and washing-up island is a central point that allows free and easy circulation.

The outstanding quality and beautiful finish can be seen in even the smallest details.

A PURE PHILOSOPHY FOR KITCHEN AND HOME DESIGN

In his dedicated search for manufacturers who could develop his ideas with a great deal of care and a high-quality finish, industrial designer Ivo de Groot found the Italian company Strato. Since then, Ivo de Groot has been the exclusive Strato distributor for Belgium. Strato's techniques and choice of materials were so close to his requirements that it was only logical that they should enter into a close collaboration. Ivo de Groot and Marco Gorini have been Strato's regular design team ever since. Their passion for kitchens has expanded in recent years to become a total vision of interior design.

www.stratobelgium.be

Work surfaces and floors in Monte Dura natural stone.

↖
The details in this kitchen
are finished in stainless steel.

HORIZONTALITY AND CLEAR-CUT LINES

Olivier Dwek, in collaboration with Julie Ruquois, created this contemporary kitchen
design during the renovation of a villa in the leafy outskirts of Brussels.
The sense of horizontality and the simple interplay of lines have been accentuated by
the furniture selected and by the long glass section providing a view of the garden.

www.olivierdwek.com

Slate surfaces with solid sink basins carved out from the stone. The cooking hobs and the extractor are situated on the central island.
The tall stainless-steel unit containing the refrigerator and storage space was designed as a freestanding block, and has access to the dining room on either side.

↖
Aluminium bar stools
from the Emeco collection
designed by Starck (at
Instore).

A SPECIALIST IN HIGH-QUALITY
KITCHEN WORK SURFACES

Over the years, Louis Culot has become a real niche player, concentrating exclusively
on the manufacture of high-quality work surfaces in granite, limestone and composite.
Louis Culot is one of the best-equipped and most technologically advanced natural-stone
suppliers on the Belgian market: computer-controlled CNC machines allow the firm to offer
durable work surfaces for competitive prices and within a reasonable period of time.

www.culot.be

The work surfaces in this kitchen, designed and created by Devaere sa, were made in white Carrara marble by Louis Culot, with a smoothed finish, and mitred to give a thickness of 5 cm.

A DISTINCTIVE NEW VILLA
IN WOODED SURROUNDINGS

This exclusive villa, situated in wooded surroundings, was recently constructed by the respected building contractor Belim Bouwteam to a design by architect Dirk Van Vlierberghe. The idyllic setting represented a particular challenge: to build a house that would suit the location. Partly thanks to the good relationship with the owners and the significant creative contribution made by the lady of the house, the result is a home that fits in perfectly with the owners' way of life. An ideal mix of old and new elements, of authenticity and cosiness, in a contemporary living environment.

www.belim.be

The kitchen is made up of stainless-steel and ebony units.

AN OPEN ORANGERY KITCHEN CUM DINING ROOM

For over seventy years, Van Overstraeten has been a renowned firm of cabinet-makers, carrying out projects throughout the whole of Belgium. Every project is made to measure and produced by experienced and enthusiastic experts using the best materials. Van Overstraeten is a family company in the truest sense of the word: flexible, customer-oriented and decent. The company has a multitude of loyal customers, including the Royal Family, who have belonged to Van Overstraeten's clientele for over a quarter of a century.

www.van-overstraeten.be

The open kitchen has been integrated into the orangery. The work surface with its built-in sink is made of Carrara marble. Behind the soft-grey painted doors are kitchen utensils and groceries. The furniture was built in the Van Overstraeten workshop.

A UNIQUE ATMOSPHERE

Country Cooking started years ago as the exclusive importer of the legendary cast-iron Nobel cooking ranges. The company later decided to develop their own kitchen line to reflect the Country Cooking vision, which is based on the idea that a kitchen can be furnished in just the same way as any other living space. The concept took shape: the Doran living kitchen was born. The right combination of furniture and colours and the integration of the appliances makes the kitchen into a pleasant and cosy living environment. Quality comes first at Country Cooking: all of the furniture is made according to traditional methods in solid pine or oak. This results in kitchens with a unique atmosphere and high levels of durability.

Respect for traditional principles does not conflict with the functional character of the contemporary kitchen. Patinated pinewood in bitter chocolate and flour white from the Doran colour collection has been selected here, in combination with end grain and aged oak.

A PASSION FOR NATURAL STONE

Desloover, a specialist company from Oudenaarde, has for years been one of the most respected Belgian suppliers of tiles and natural stone. In this home, designed by architect Bernard De Clerck, the company from East Flanders shows how important natural stone and tiles are in ensuring the success of a construction project.

www.desloover.com   info@bernarddeclerck.be

In the kitchen, traditional tiles have been combined with perfect custom-built work in natural stone.

PERFECTION IN CUSTOM-FITTED NATURAL STONE

This is a creation by Villabouw Sels and their interior architect Steven Van Dooren.
All of the work in natural stone has been carried out by Van den Weghe.

www.sels.be   www.vandenweghe.be

In the kitchen, aged Buxy Gris / Jaune / Cendré has been chosen, in combination with work surfaces and sinks in Bianco Statuario: a very hard white marble used by sculptors including Michelangelo. The area above the stove has been tiled with zeliges.

SHADES OF GREEN

In this kitchen, architect Stéphane Boens created a daring blend of green shades (for the cupboards) with orange linen (for the chairs) and old white Carrara marble floors.

www.stephaneboens.be

A Lacanche cooker.

OLD AND NEW

Both old and new elements have been used in this kitchen by am projects.
On the dining table is a 'grasshopper' lamp from the Actuals collection.

www.amprojects.be

Floor coverings: reclaimed tiles in Carrara marble and a solid oak planks.

THE REAL CENTRE OF THE HOUSE

This kitchen, designed and realized by Sphere Concepts, is the real heart of the house.

www.sphereconcepts.be

Kitchen block with barstools by Piet Boon. Hanging lamps by Stéphane Davidts. Units in composite stone. The wall behind the cooker is clad with Moroccan zeliges.

The floor of the wine cellar is made of old factory bricks. Wine niches in French white stone. The walls have been treated using an old lime technique. Table in old teak and a traditionally made wrought-iron gate.

THE REVIVAL OF A 19TH-CENTURY CASTLE

This distinctive castle, which was used as a country seat by different generations of noble families, underwent a painstaking restoration a few years ago. The nineteenth-century castle, situated on an estate of five hectares with ancient trees and a variety of ponds in an English landscape style, was bombed during World War I and rebuilt after the war. The present owners restored their historic home in close collaboration with architect Stéphane Boens.

www.stephaneboens.be

Floors and worktops in
Carrara marble. A La Cornue
cooking unit.

FRESHENING UP
A RESTORED FARMHOUSE

This 19th-century farmhouse with a courtyard has been
freshened up and given a more contemporary feel.
Original elements were retained as far as possible, and nothing
about the existing structure of the house was changed: a gentle renovation.

www.obumex.be   info@annickgrimmelprez.be

The floor of the kitchen and dining area is in Pietra di Medici slabs (120x80 cm). The original beams have been whitewashed. Elm table and chairs (covered with Libeco linen) from am projects. Wooden block and lamp by Liaigre. Lighting in the beams by Mexcal (from Kurve).

↖
The kitchen was created by Obumex, partly in white-painted MDF, partly in bleached oak.

RENOVATION OF AN 18TH-CENTURY MILL

Interior architect Catherine Verbeke and her husband fell in love with an 18th-century mill. They contacted architect Baudouin Courtens to transform the small pieces into a spacious and inviting living area, with beautiful garden views.

www.courtens.be

The walk-through kitchen, with warm/cold contrasts in stainless steel and rough wood, joins the front and back gardens.

CREATING THE PERFECT KITCHEN

Frank Tack's kitchens are always full of character and sophistication. They have a timeless atmosphere and are very pleasant spaces in which not just to cook, but also to eat, to work and to entertain. Each piece of furniture designed by Tack is unique and made with great skill in the most luxurious of materials. Whether the project involves a classic, country kitchen or a more streamlined look, Tack ensures a close connection between the design and the creation, carefully matching the client's wishes to the final result. Frank Tack's kitchens are always a special experience: a blend of genuine cosiness and joie de vivre.

www.tack-keukens.be

Cosy and convivial, but harmonious and functional too:
every kitchen by Frank Tack has many facets.

COLONIAL INSPIRATION

This kitchen in a colonial atmosphere, designed by Filip Vanryckeghem and created by Vandeputte bvba from Proven (Poperinge), is part of the complete renovation of a ground-floor apartment in Brussels. The designer did away with the traditional layout and the old-fashioned character of the rooms, introducing a new, contemporary look.

www.ixtra.be

The work surfaces in smooth composite stone harmonise
with the rougher look of the ceramic floor tiles.
The distinctive panels on all of the cupboard units are finished
with a top layer of solid beech in a dark patina.

RELIABLE AND FUNCTIONAL

A reliable, functional kitchen was essential for the owners of this old farmhouse. Cooking and experimenting with new, exquisite ingredients is a passion for them, so they needed top-quality equipment: oven, combi-steamer, warming drawer and induction hob, all by Gaggenau. The large fridge-freezer is by Viking and the taps are by Dornbracht.

www.demenagerie.be

This compact kitchen – simple, convenient and very cosy – is built in oak veneer with an almost black finish – noir brûlé – and fronts with no handles. The cooking island, with a surface in Buxy stone, enjoys a view of the garden.

AUTHENTIC CHARM

This open kitchen, designed and realized by De Menagerie, has authentic charm.
The worktops in smoothed bluestone, the washbasin was handcut from a massive stone.
A wall mounted Volevatch tap, a Falcon cooker and an Amana refrigerator.

www.demenagerie.be

EXCLUSIVE KITCHENS WITH
A CONTEMPORARY EDGE

Liedssen has been a leading kitchen manufacturer for over thirty years. All of the designs are made and installed by Liedssen after close consultation with the client. Each project is unique, but they are all characterised by their elegant and timeless appeal. Liedssen's focus is on creating a harmonious look with a streamlined design and a top-quality finish, based on durable materials and kitchen equipment.

www.liedssen.be

This open kitchen/dining room is in aged, sandblasted oak with concealed handles. The grain of the wood is vertical, emphasising the high ceiling. The 5cm-thick flamed bluestone work surface matches the floor tiles. The kitchen island contains an induction hob and a Gaggenau extractor that is concealed within the counter. This warm, timeless design has a wonderfully cosy atmosphere, created in part by the open fireplace in the sitting area.

Liedssen created this project, which was designed by Paris architect Maxime d'Angeac. This functional, user-friendly kitchen is in oak with a dark stain. The stainless-steel work surfaces have a satin finish. The kitchen island is a central pole around which the activity flows.

THE KITCHEN AS THE CORE
OF A HOME-DESIGN CONCEPT

Doran for Country Cooking builds complete interiors in a streamlined or country style, placing the kitchen at the centre of the design concept. Traditional craftsmanship is always an essential element of these designs. The company creates customised solutions for every aspect of life at home, from living rooms to bathrooms, from bedrooms to dressing rooms. A balance between functionality and aesthetics is the key to a successful interior design. The distinctive villa in this report is a fine example of the company's philosophy, which results in a unique atmosphere in every room.

A kitchen with a Godin stove.
Furniture in solid wood, with
work surfaces in Belgian
bluestone.
Traditional wall tiles from the
Doran collection. Floor tiles
in natural stone from Doran's
Fleur de Lys collection.

This grand orangery creates
a harmonious connection
between the living room and
the kitchen.

THE COOKER AS THE HEART OF THE KITCHEN

For over a quarter of a century, Alfa Belgium / Bis has been the exclusive importer of the legendary Aga cookers in Belgium and Luxembourg. Alfa Belgium / Bis also won the right a few years ago to import the top-quality French La Cornue cookers into Belgium: this was a new development for this family company from Ghent, which within twenty-five years has become the port of call for advice on all three top-quality brands of cooker.

www.aga.be

The decision was taken for a Le Grand Châtelet 135 model from La Cornue.
It is possible to combine three or four cooking elements to match your own preferences, including a grate, on the heavy stainless steel cooking bench (on gas, electric, or a combination).

The sober and robust Aga (here in the four-oven version) fits very well in this kitchen created by Francis Van Damme. The dining room and chimney lambris are by Bart Speck.

Recently Aga presented an innovation: the AIMS system (Aga Intelligent Management System) with which electric Aga cookers can be equipped. With this, users can coordinate the latent temperature in their Aga with their personal way of life and their presence in the kitchen. It is in fact a programme that is, moreover, very user-friendly.

CREATIVITY AND CRAFTSMANSHIP

Fahrenheit is the cooking shop par excellence. The company designs kitchens and distributes stoves and other professional and semi-professional kitchen equipment from its salesrooms on Louizalaan in Brussels, where top-quality kitchen accessories are also available. Owner Thierry Goffin has developed a unique concept of "culinary ergonomics": the kitchen is not simply a nice space, but is a real "living room", where cooking is an absolute pleasure. Top professionals ensure the design of the perfect kitchen, built in the best of materials and equipped with appliances of the highest standard.

www.fahrenheit.be

The owners asked Thierry Goffin to design a classic shelf unit in the dining room to display their outstanding collection of French, Belgian and Portuguese barbotine pottery. The soft light behind the shelves gives this pale-grey room a very pleasant warmth and cosiness.

This dresser is in hand-blown glass and painted tulipwood. It offers sufficient space to display both the beautiful Villeroy & Boch porcelain service and the family coat of arms. A number of long-lasting, high-efficiency LEDs in warm colours illuminate the glass display section.

Kitchen and dining room form a whole beneath this authentic 18th-century beam. with a large sitting room and open fireplace behind.
Thierry Goffin worked with a craftsman from Liège to create a padded barstool to match the height of the island. The finish of the stools shows
the unparalleled classic elegance of this furniture.

BIANCO STATUARIO IN THE KITCHEN

This report features Bianco Statuario marble in two recent kitchen projects in very different styles: one in a classic country setting and the other in a streamlined, contemporary kitchen. Van den Weghe (The Stone Company) created both of these kitchens. The exclusive white marble is one of company director Philippe Van den Weghe's favourite types of stone. It is one of the most highly regarded marbles and comes from the world-famous quarries of Carrara in Italy, which also supplied the stone for Michelangelo's sculptures.

www.vandenweghe.be

In this Themenos project, Bianco Statuario marble is used as an exclusive and hardwearing kitchen work surface, created by Van den Weghe (The Stonecompany).
The flagstones on the floor are by Rik Storms.

These sinks were carved from solid Bianco Statuario marble.
Michelangelo knew all about this versatile and exclusive stone.

This project by architect Axel Verbeke illustrates how Bianco Statuario can be used to great effect in a contemporary context. The combination of white marble and an aged oak floor creates a very cosy look, with clean lines.

THE RESTORATION OF THE HISTORIC
CRETENBURGHOEVE

The Cretenburghoeve is a listed building dating back to the eighteenth century (1771). The building had fallen into disrepair and urgent restoration was needed to prevent collapse. Pas-partoe interiors took care of the work inside the farmhouse, while architect K. Beeck, a specialist in the restoration of historic buildings, coordinated the exterior work. Ballmore landscaped the garden. Pas-partoe created a bright, open home, which has a simple appearance, yet uses classic, high-quality materials. The company created clean views through the building by concealing any elements, such as radiators, that might disturb the lines.

www.pas-partoe.be

Sandblasted oak is combined with smooth bluestone in the kitchen. A large sliding panel conceals the kitchen appliances. The custom-made table is based on a design by pas-partoe.

The organic form of the "Tulip" chairs by Eero Saarinen contrasts with the straight lines of the fitted kitchen units and table.

EPISCOPAL INSPIRATION

This residence for a family with three growing children was built by architect Bernard De Clerck in a classic eighteenth-century style: he drew his inspiration from a bishop's country seat near Bruges, which dates back to 1750. The quality of the light, the creation of perspectives and the optimal orientation of the rooms were important in the design of this house. All the spaces are arranged around an inner courtyard, which means that the occupants can enjoy the sunlight in different rooms for most of the day.

info@bernarddeclerck.be

The kitchen, with a view through to the everyday dining room and the sitting room (on the left-hand side).
The floor is laid with old white stone and Belgian bluestone.
The hood above the Aga stove is clad with decorative stuccowork. In the background is a view through to the oak-panelled back entrance hall.

ANNO 1642

This house, dating back to 1642, with its four bays and saddleback roof in the traditional brick and sandstone style and its abutting nineteenth-century buildings, has been restored and radically re-modelled by architect Bernard De Clerck to make it a fully fledged contemporary home for a family with three young children. The owners wished to put all the rooms to their best use, enjoying the magnificent surroundings and making use of the natural light, orientation and straightforward materials such as stone, wood and whitewash. This is a house that radiates peace and simplicity, in perfect harmony with the untouched landscape with its old orchard.

info@bernarddeclerck.be

The iron window opens outward completely and gives this room the feeling of a covered spot outdoors. The floor is made of old bricks.

The fittings in the scullery have been built in and provided with old doors. The taps are reclaimed.

INTIMATE AND COSY

This very inviting kitchen with fireplace and living area has been designed by Themenos.

www.themenos.be

MINIMALISM AND CONTEMPORARY ART

In this city apartment Olivier Dwek created an essentialist
kitchen for a collector of contemporary art.
The kitchen design is by Bulthaup. Architect Coline Visse also collaborated in this project.

www.olivierdwek.com

Worktop in white Corian (13 mm thin). The door panels have been lacquered white. The cooker hood is in brushed stainless steel and glass. Artwork «Clown mirror» by Roni Horn (gallery Xavier Hufkens).

A PERFECT ERGONOMY

Fahrenheit, the Brussels kitchen designer and cook shop, has
created this kitchen with perfect ergonomy.

www.fahrenheit.be

A RECENTLY BUILT COUNTRY HOUSE
WITH AN AGE-OLD PATINA

Although the country house in this report was constructed only recently, it seems to have a patina of great age. This is not only the result of the consistent use of weathered and reclaimed materials on the exterior, the interior also has a timeless, historic atmosphere. Dankers Decor, who have a royal warrant and are one of the most renowned Belgian decorating companies, created a harmony of colours throughout the whole house, using Arte Constructo's lime paints, coloured with natural pigments: an "à la carte" solution for this beautiful house.

www.arteconstructo.be

On the floor, antique tiles in Carrara marble.

↖
The fitted oak cupboards
have an aged lime finish.
In the centre, a La
Cornue stove.

PUBLISHER
BETA-PLUS publishing
www.betaplus.com

PHOTOGRAPHY
Jo Pauwels

DESIGN
Polydem – Nathalie Binart

ISBN : 978-90-8944-111-9

Coordination production printing and binding :
www.belvedere.nl - André Kloppenberg
Printing and binding: Printer Trento, Italy